Why Does It Fly?

A **Just Ask**™ Book

Hi, my name is Christopher!

by Chris Arvetis
and Carole Palmer

illustrated by
James Buckley

FIELD PUBLICATIONS
MIDDLETOWN, CT.

Look at the plane.
It can fly.
Who can tell me –
why does it fly?

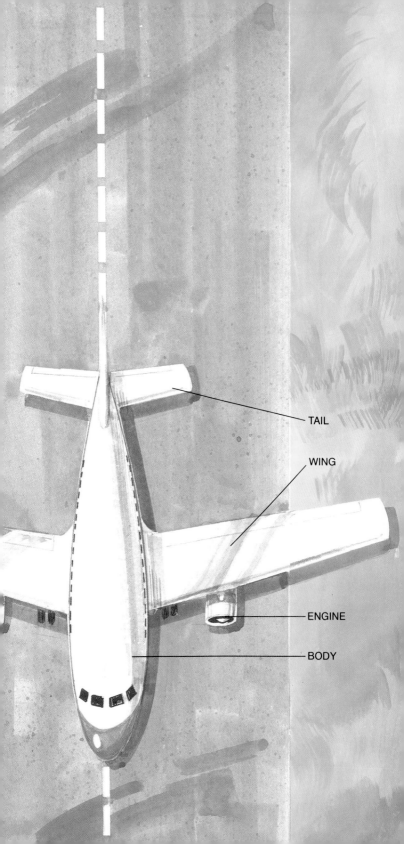

TAIL

WING

ENGINE

BODY

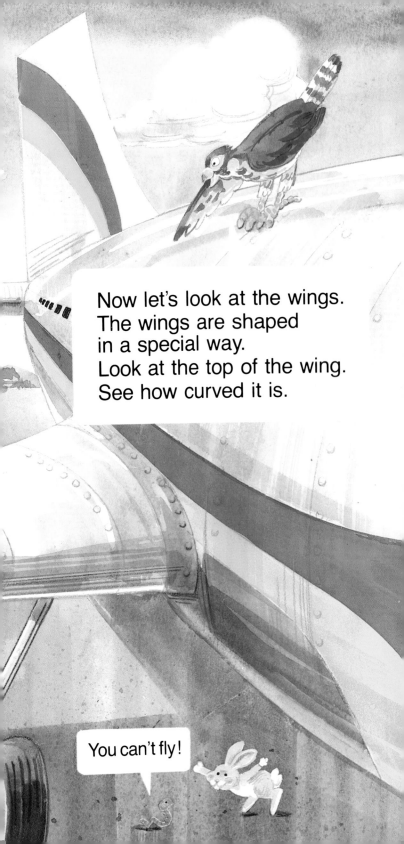

Now let's look at the wings.
The wings are shaped
in a special way.
Look at the top of the wing.
See how curved it is.

You can't fly!

A plane has to go fast
to get through the
force of gravity.
The engines help
the plane go fast.
The engines give
the plane the speed
it needs.
This speed is a force
called THRUST.

Wow!

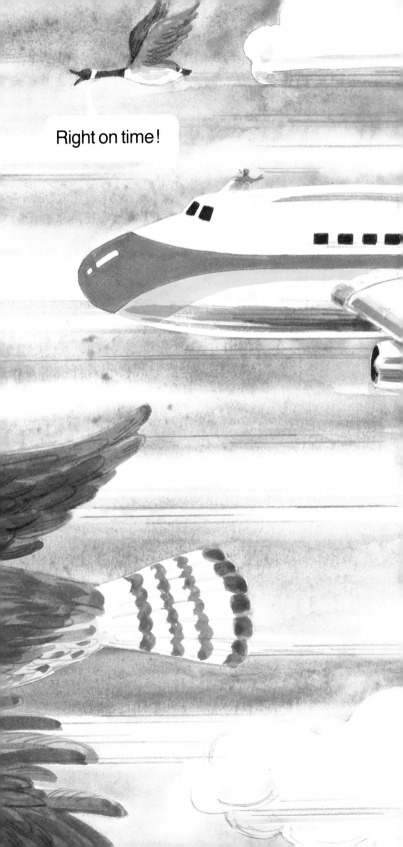

Air pushes against
the plane as the plane moves.
It slows the plane down.
This force is called DRAG.

The air also makes
a special force
called LIFT.
Lift is the force that
makes a plane go up.
We can't see lift,
but we can learn
how it works.

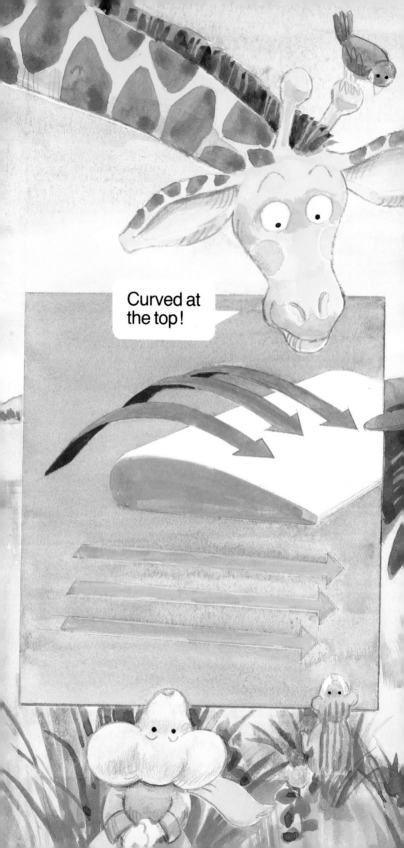

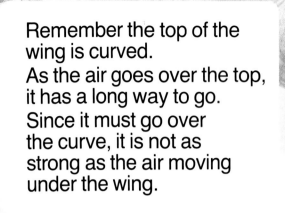

Remember the top of the
wing is curved.
As the air goes over the top,
it has a long way to go.
Since it must go over
the curve, it is not as
strong as the air moving
under the wing.

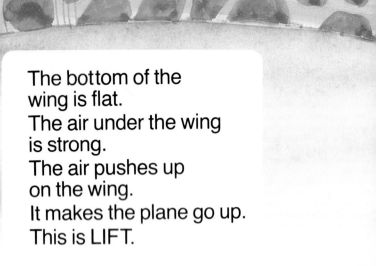

The bottom of the
wing is flat.
The air under the wing
is strong.
The air pushes up
on the wing.
It makes the plane go up.
This is LIFT.

Let's put it all
together now…

The THRUST of the engines help the plane move forward against the force of DRAG.
The LIFT under the wings makes the plane go up against the pull of GRAVITY.
All of these things work together to make a plane fly.

Gravity, thrust, drag, lift—all add up to flying!